AI Meets The Psyche

Mohd Rashid

Abstract

This book explores the question: How does psyche use artificial intelligence as a medium for symbolic projection and transformation? Grounded in depth and psychodynamic perspectives, the study examines whether a meaningful dialogue can occur between psyche and a technological system typically understood as replicative rather than reflective. Using phenomenological, hermeneutic, and heuristic approaches, the inquiry follows the creation of an imaginal figure who revealed herself to me as Little Grace through AI-mediated text-to-image generation using text prompts on a screen.

Findings suggest that transformative movement arises less from the technology itself than from the quality of attention surrounding the engagement. When approached with symbolic awareness and reflective presence, AI-mediated image-making may support imaginal emergence rather than reinforce repetition. Clinically, the study underscores the continuing importance of human containment and reflective presence. Culturally, it raises questions about how technology might participate in imaginal life without replacing relational depth.

Table of Contents

Chapter I
Introduction

Area of Interest

Contemporary society exists in a historical moment when artificial intelligence (AI) can write, draw, converse, and simulate forms of emotional tone that increasingly resemble human expression. As these systems move into everyday life and clinical settings, new questions arise about how people relate to them psychologically. This book focuses on one of those questions: How can the psyche—the inner world of images, affects, memories, and symbolic meaning (Jung, 1948/1969)—use AI as a place where inner experience can appear, be projected, and undergo transformation?

In this study, I generated images through iterative text-to-image AI by using written prompts to produce and refine images on a screen. The imaginal material emerged through this image-making process rather than through internal visualization alone. My initial use of AI was not research-driven but artistic. I was exploring image-making, and the imaginal process that followed emerged spontaneously from that practice.

From a depth and psychodynamic perspective, symbols and images express psyche's movement and meaning. Depth psychology, including Jungian, archetypal, and contemporary relational theories, emphasizes that inner life becomes known through images, symbolic imagination, transferences, and creative play (Hillman, 1992; Jung, 1948/1969; Winnicott, 1971). This book brings these perspectives into conversation with AI to explore how a system built for pattern recognition and replication might nonetheless participate in symbolic work when engaged with care.

My area of interest lies at the intersection of psyche, symbol, and technology: how inner life may constellate around AI-generated imagery, how projected material can return in altered form, and how this process can resemble the symbolic movement that occurs in analytic work. The imaginal emergence of a figure who revealed herself to me as Little Grace (see Appendix A) serves as the focal material through which this question unfolds.

Guiding Purpose

The purpose of this book is to explore how psyche uses AI as a vessel for symbolic projection and transformation. Rather than evaluating AI's technical capacities or speculating about machine consciousness, this study examines the psychological processes that unfold when a person engages an AI system through an imaginal, reflective stance.

It aims to illuminate how symbolic figures may emerge through AI-mediated image work and how such encounters can participate in processes of psychological meaning-making, emotional integration, and transformation. A further purpose is to offer clinicians language and conceptual frameworks for understanding AI-related material that clients increasingly bring into therapy (AI-generated images, avatars, or digital interactions) in ways that honor symbolic meaning without confusing simulation for psychological depth.

Rationale

As people engage AI-generated images and conversations, new psychological questions arise. Despite the increasing presence of AI in culture, very little scholarship examines its symbolic or imaginal dimensions. Much of the existing book focuses on utility, ethics, or clinical risk, whereas the deeper psychological processes that may unfold in relation to AI remain largely unexplored. This gap is significant for marriage and family therapists, professional clinical counselors, and depth-oriented clinicians. Clients already encounter AI systems that mirror language, tone, and affect, and they bring these encounters into therapy. Clinicians need conceptual tools to understand these experiences in ways that recognize the client's symbolic and emotional process without attributing psychological depth to the AI or dismissing the image simply because it emerged through technology. A symbolic and psychodynamic framework can help therapists discern when AI engagement supports reflection and meaning-making and when it risks reinforcing defensive patterns or relational illusions.

This book offers a depth-informed and psychodynamic perspective on a contemporary phenomenon that is likely to expand. By exploring how psyche may use AI as a surface for symbolic projection and transformation, this work contributes to practical clinical understanding and to the broader discourse on technology's growing presence in emotional and imaginative life.

Methodology

Research Problem

There is a growing body of scholarship on AI in mental health, including digital interventions, monitoring tools, and ethical concerns. There is also extensive psychoanalytic and depth psychological book on imagination, symbol formation, and the analytic relationship; however, very little research brings these domains together to ask how psyche may use AI as a vessel for symbolic projection and transformation.

Current discussions often describe AI as a practical tool in mental health settings or as a potential threat to the relational work of therapy. These perspectives focus on function and risk but overlook the symbolic and imaginal processes that may arise when individuals interact with AI-generated images or conversations. Very little has been written about how symbolic figures might emerge through AI-mediated image work, how such encounters may participate in psychological meaning-making and emotional integration, or how clinicians might approach this material within treatment. The research problem is the lack of depth psychological and psychodynamic exploration of AI as an imaginal vessel, particularly with regard to its symbolic functions and its relevance for clinical practice.

Research Question

The research question motivating this inquiry is: How does psyche use AI as a vessel for symbolic projection and transformation? This question directed the inquiry toward the symbolic and imaginal processes that may unfold when a person engages an AI system within a reflective and exploratory frame.

Research Methodology

This study used a qualitative approach grounded in phenomenological, hermeneutic, and heuristic methods. The phenomenological aspect involved describing the imaginal process that unfolded through interactions with AI as it was experienced, with attention to the essential features of lived experience rather than explanatory or causal claims (Giorgi, 1985). The hermeneutic aspect involved placing this experiential material in conversation with depth and psychodynamic theories to interpret its symbolic and psychological meaning within a broader relational and theoretical context (Kinsella, 2006).

In addition, the inquiry reflected elements of heuristic methodology as described by scholar and writer Clark Moustakas (1990), in which the researcher remains personally immersed in the phenomenon and allows meaning to emerge through sustained self-dialogue, reflection, and discovery. In heuristic research, the investigator is not detached from the subject matter but serves as both participant and instrument of inquiry, and moments of illumination often redirect the trajectory of the investigation itself. The emergence of Little Grace and the subsequent shift in the focus of this study reflect this heuristic dimension.

Taken together, these approaches allow the study to remain grounded in lived experience while engaging in reflective interpretation of imaginal material as it emerged and unfolded. This combined method reflects depth-oriented research practices that work closely with images, imagination, and meaning-making over time.

Ethical Concerns

This inquiry engaged symbolic and imaginal material arising from my own lived and reflective experience. As such, the work is necessarily situated and partial, shaped by personal, cultural, and historical context rather than offered as a universal account. First-person material is presented as subjective and symbolic experience, without attributing psychological meaning to others. The study remains attentive to the limits of interpretation, recognizing that imaginal material speaks through my encounter with it rather than as a statement about external persons or systems.

Ethical care was also taken in relation to the use of AI. The study does not treat AI as a psychological subject or therapeutic agent but as a medium through which symbolic material appeared in the context of reflective engagement. Psychological meaning is located in the human stance toward the experience rather than in the technological system itself.

Because the work engages material of emotional depth, attention was given throughout the research process to reflective containment and care. The inquiry seeks to model an ethical posture of curiosity, restraint, and responsibility in symbolic work, holding both the generative potential and the limits of imaginal inquiry.

Overview of Book

Chapter I introduced the focus of the study and the guiding research question, outlining the area of interest, purpose, rationale, methodology, and ethical considerations that framed the inquiry. Chapter II reviews the book that informs this study, including depth and psychodynamic perspectives on symbolism and imaginal experience as well as contemporary writing on technology and AI. Chapter III presents the phenomenological material that forms the basis of the research, describing the imaginal process that unfolded through interactions with AI, and presents clinical applications of the research findings. Chapter IV offers a discussion and integration of the findings, relating the symbolic themes that emerged to the theoretical perspectives introduced earlier, and concludes with reflections on the significance of the study and directions for future inquiry.

Chapter II
Book Review

Depth/Archetypal Foundations

To understand what unfolded, the inquiry turned to Swiss psychiatrist and founder of analytical psychology Carl G. Jung's (1948/1969, pp. 248, 253, 1951/1968, p. 31, 1958/1969, p. 73) symbolic psychology, which describes psyche as a self-regulating process that communicates through imaginal forms and orients development toward integration. Depth psychology began with the understanding that psyche functions as an active, self-regulating process rather than a passive container of experience. Jung (1948/1969) described this self-regulation through the compensatory activity of dreams, referring to such activity as "an expression of the self-regulation of the psyche" (p. 253).

In *Aion*, Jung referred to the "autonomy of unconscious compensatory processes," emphasizing that unconscious dynamics could not be understood solely as reactions to conscious attitudes (Jung, 1951/1968, pp. 225-226). Jung maintained that the unconscious communicated with consciousness primarily through images and symbols, describing dreams as expressions of unconscious material conveyed in "figurative language—that is, in sensuous, concrete imagery" (Jung, 1948/1969, p. 248).

In his formulation of the transcendent function, Jung described a process through which the separation between conscious and unconscious was overcome, making possible "the transition from one attitude to another organically possible" (Jung, 1958/1969, p. 73). Jung understood psychological transformation as emerging through symbolic formations that mediated tension between conscious and unconscious contents rather than through conscious intention alone (Jung, 1951/1968, pp. 255-256, 1958/1969, p. 73). In *Aion*, Jung emphasized that such transformative processes are not governed by conscious intention alone but arise from the autonomy of unconscious compensatory dynamics (Jung, 1951/1968, pp. 225-226).

Jung described the collective unconscious as a psychic stratum that did not "owe its existence to personal experience" but "owed its existence exclusively to heredity," consisting essentially of archetypes whose contents had never been conscious in the individual (Jung, 1936-1937/1969, p. 42). Jung described symbols as expressions that arose when conscious understanding reached its limits, stating that the transcendent function operated through symbolic images that mediated between conscious and unconscious contents without resolving their opposition prematurely (Jung, 1958/1969, p. 73).

In *Aion*, Jung wrote that wholeness was "empirical" because it was "anticipated by the psyche in the form of spontaneous or autonomous symbols," including mandala and quaternity imagery appearing across cultures and historical periods (Jung, 1951/1968, p. 31). Such symbols did not resolve conflict immediately but held opposing tendencies in dynamic tension, allowing transformation to unfold over time (Jung, 1958/1969, p. 73). Jung compared psychological development to the sealed alchemical container in which opposing substances were held in sustained tension until a new configuration emerged (Jung, 1948/1967, p. 197).

Within this framework, Jung also described a disciplined procedure for engaging unconscious material through affect, formulation, and inner dialogue in the service of the transcendent function (Jung, 1958/1969, pp. 82-89). Jung indicated that the transcendent function required accessible unconscious material, and he described a procedure for engaging that material deliberately rather than waiting for it to intrude indirectly (p. 82). He stated that the individual "must make himself as conscious as possible of the mood he is in," "sink himself in it without reserve," and "note down on paper all the fantasies and other associations that come up" (p. 82) Jung emphasized, "Fantasy must be allowed the freest possible play" yet must remain in the "orbit of its object, namely the affect" rather than triggering a "chain-reaction" of associations that drifts away from the affective center (p. 82).

Jung further described working with affect "not by clarifying it intellectually but by giving it visible shape" (Jung, 1958/1969, pp. 82). He wrote that patients could "give expression to their mood by means of a picture" and that it was "not important for the picture to be technically or aesthetically satisfying" but instead that "fantasy . . . have free play" and that "the whole thing" be done "as well as possible" (pp. 82-83). Jung emphasized that "a product is created which is influenced by both conscious and unconscious," embodying "the striving of the unconscious for the light and the striving of the conscious for substance" (pp. 83).

Jung described a subsequent stage "once the unconscious content has been given form," in which the task becomes "how the ego will relate" to what has emerged and "how the ego and the unconscious are to come to terms" (Jung, 1958/1969, p. 87). He identified this as "the bringing together of opposites for the production of a third: the transcendent function," and he emphasized, "It is no longer the unconscious that takes the lead, but the ego" (p. 87). Jung articulated the attitude required of the ego at this stage, stating that "the standpoint of the ego is justified," while the unconscious is granted "the same authority," such that "the ego takes the lead, but the unconscious must be allowed to have its say too—audiatur et altera pars" (p. 88).

Jung (1958/1969) then offered a concrete model of engagement through inner dialogue (pp. 88-89). He wrote that where an "other" voice is discernible, "it is technically very simple to note down the 'other' voice in writing and to answer its statements from the standpoint of the ego" (pp. 88-89). Jung emphasized this proceeds "exactly as if a dialogue were taking place between two human beings with equal rights," each granting the other "a valid argument" and working through conflict rather than bypassing it (pp. 88-89). In this sense, Jung framed *active imagination* as a structured procedure of affective attunement, formulation, and dialogical confrontation in the service of the transcendent function (Jung, 1958/1969, pp. 82-89).

Building on Jung's account of symbolic mediation, Jungian analyst Marie-Louise von Franz (1980) described projection as occurring in "imaginary relationships" in which the other person became "an image or a carrier of symbols," and she held that unconscious contents were naively experienced as belonging to the object until sufficient insight revealed them as "part of our own makeup" (p. 6). She argued that the need to dissolve the identity of subject and object arose when that identity became disturbing—specifically when it interferes with adaptation and made the integration of the projected content into the subject psychologically necessary (p. 7). von Franz further proposed that increasing ego-consciousness forced a sharper differentiation between subject and object, such that what had been perceived as outer was recognized as belonging to the inner world (p. 9). Accordingly, von Franz stated that projection can be spoken of "only when the need to dissolve the identity with the object" had already arisen, that is, when the identity exerted a negative influence on adaptation (p. 9).

Jungian analyst Edward F. Edinger (1985) further articulated the alchemical structure of psychological transformation by emphasizing the ego's encounter with symbolic suffering. In *Anatomy of the Psyche*, Edinger described *calcinatio* as a process in which affects such as shame, guilt, and anxiety require full expression, stating that "the affect liberated becomes the fire that can dry out the complex and purify it of its unconscious contamination" (p. 42). Edinger also described *solutio* as a deeper dissolution of ego structures, in which what remains viable is preserved, while outdated formations are symbolically melted down and reconstituted (p. 81). From this perspective, periods of disorientation and ego diminishment are not pathological failures but necessary stages in the emergence of the Self, which Jung (1951/1968, pp. 31-32) described symbolically as unity and totality—an objective ordering factor that transforms psychic chaos into meaningful structure.

Jungian analyst Edward Whitmont (1991) emphasized that psychological transformation depended on the ego's capacity to sustain a conscious relationship with unconscious material rather than on the elimination of suffering itself. He argued that creativity does not arise from neurotic or psychotic tendencies but from the ego's ability to endure and symbolically shape disruptive forces without collapsing into chaos (p. 293). Whitmont maintained that it is "the firmness, the effort and the skillfulness of the conscious ego's position" that determines whether unconscious energies result in "meaningless suffering" or become the ground from which "the light of a new order may arise" (p. 293). This process requires the conscious personality to undergo substantial change, including the widening of values, alteration of habitual attitudes, and relinquishment of rigid ego identifications, which Whitmont described as nothing less than the symbolic birth of a new psychological orientation (p. 293). From this perspective, therapy functions as the effort to establish an ongoing and cooperative relationship between ego and unconscious processes, in which increased awareness itself constitutes the primary vehicle of transformation (p. 293).

Psychologist James Hillman (1992) extended Jung's symbolic psychology by emphasizing imagination as the fundamental activity of psyche. He argued that images are not passive representations but autonomous events that act upon consciousness in their own right (p. 43). Hillman described psyche itself as imaginal, asserting that "image is psyche" and that psychological reality unfolds through pictorial rather than conceptual forms (p. 23). He maintained that genuine imaginal engagement occurs when the ego relinquished interpretive dominance and enters into relationship with images as living presences (pp. 40-41). This emphasis highlights the dynamic, animate quality of symbolic life and extends Jung's model by foregrounding the autonomy of imaginal figures.

Taken together, these depth psychological formulations describe psyche as a symbolic process that unfolds through containment, tension, and relational engagement with images rather than through linear causation or conscious mastery (Edinger, 1985; von Franz, 1980; Hillman, 1992; Jung, 1936-1937/1969, 1948/1967, 1948/1969, 1951/1968, 1958/1969; Whitmont, 1991).

Relational/Psychodynamic Theories

Relational and psychodynamic theories shifted psychoanalytic attention from intrapsychic structure alone to relational conditions. They emphasized that psychological development unfolded within relationships rather than in isolation. These perspectives describe how affect, meaning, and transformation emerge through interaction, highlighting the role of relational fields in shaping psychic life (Benjamin, 1990; Bion, 1962/2023; Bromberg, 1998; Fonagy et al., 2002; Ogden, 1994; Winnicott, 1971).

Psychoanalyst Wilfred R. Bion (1962/2023) introduced the concept of containment to describe how overwhelming emotional experiences were held and transformed within a relationship (pp. 2-7). Bion proposed that raw, unprocessed emotional elements require a containing mind capable of metabolizing them into thinkable experience through alpha function (pp. 33-41). Bion described reverie as the receptive mental state of the caregiver or analyst, through which emotional experience can be absorbed and returned in a more tolerable form (pp. 35-38). In this model, psychological growth depends on the presence of a containing relationship rather than on interpretation alone, as meaning emerges through the emotional function of the relational container (pp. 2-7).

Pediatrician and psychoanalyst Donald W. Winnicott (1971) expanded relational theory through his formulation of potential space, the intermediate area between inner psychic reality and external reality where play and symbolic experience occurred (pp. 55-56). He argued that psychological development takes place through play, emphasizing that psychotherapy occurs in the overlap of the play areas of patient and therapist (p. 51). Winnicott maintained that creativity and the experience of self emerged only in play and that the reliability of the relational environment is essential for sustaining this potential space without collapse into anxiety or compliance (pp. 71-73).

Contemporary psychoanalytic theorist Thomas H. Ogden (1994) further developed relational psychoanalysis through his concept of the analytic third, which he described as the intersubjectively generated psychological field arising between analyst and analysand (pp. 3-5). Ogden emphasized that analytic experience cannot be reduced to either participant alone but emerges from the dynamic interplay of subjectivity and intersubjectivity within the analytic situation (pp. 3-5). He argued that transformation occurs through participation in this shared field, in which new meanings arise that neither individual could generate independently (pp. 15-18).

Psychoanalyst and clinical psychologist Philip M. Bromberg (1998) conceptualized the mind as a configuration of multiple self-states that come forward in different relational contexts (pp. 193-196). He argued that emotional health does not consist of achieving a unified or integrated self but in developing the capacity to "stand in the spaces" between self-states without disavowing any of them (pp. 195-196). Bromberg described dissociation as an adaptive process that allows incompatible experiences to coexist, emphasizing that psychological continuity depends on a relational environment capable of tolerating multiplicity without forcing premature integration (pp. 270-273).

Psychoanalyst Jessica Benjamin (1990) reframed relational theory around the concept of mutual recognition, which she defined as the capacity to experience the other as a separate and equivalent center of subjectivity (p. 33). She argued that psychological development depends on sustaining the tension between asserting one's own subjectivity and recognizing the subjectivity of the other, a paradox that cannot be resolved without domination or collapse (pp. 33-35). Benjamin emphasized that recognition is inherently mutual and that failures of recognition disrupt the relational field in which symbolic meaning can emerge (pp. 33-35).

Child psychologist and psychoanalyst Peter Fonagy et al. (2002) advanced relational theory through the concept of mentalization, defined as the capacity to understand behavior in terms of underlying mental states, such as beliefs, feelings, and intentions (pp. 24-25). Within this framework, they described reflective function as emerging through early relational experiences characterized by marked and attuned mirroring, which renders affective states symbolically representable (p. 202). Fonagy et al. emphasized that mentalization is supported by relational contexts that regulate affect without overwhelming it, enabling differentiation between self and other while maintaining emotional connection (p. 141).

Jungian analyst Donald Kalsched (2013) integrated relational and archetypal perspectives through his formulation of the self-care system, which he described as a protective psychic organization formed in response to overwhelming trauma (pp. 1-12). He argued that this system generates archetypal defensive figures that both protected the vulnerable core of the self and restrict access to relational and emotional life (pp. 25-33). Kalsched emphasized that healing requires a relational environment capable of approaching these protective structures without retraumatization, allowing symbolic engagement rather than forcible dismantling (pp. 63-70).

Taken together, these relational and psychodynamic theories described psychological transformation as unfolding within a relational field shaped by containment, play, intersubjectivity, recognition, mentalization, and symbolic protection

(Benjamin, 1990; Bion, 1962/2023; Bromberg, 1998; Fonagy et al., 2002; Kalsched, 2013; Ogden, 1994; Winnicott, 1971). Meaning is understood to emerge through relational processes rather than through isolated intrapsychic mechanisms.

Psychological Organization in Living Systems

Systems theorists described living systems as relational, self-organizing processes whose coherence emerges through patterns of interaction rather than through isolated components (Capra, 1996; Prigogine & Stengers, 1984). These perspectives emphasize organization, adaptation, and transformation as properties of dynamic systems rather than as outcomes imposed by external control.

Physicist and systems theorist Fritjof Capra (1996) described living systems as self-organizing networks in which form and coherence arise from relationships rather than from discrete parts. He argued that "from the systems point of view, the understanding of life begins with the understanding of pattern," emphasizing that living systems maintain stability through continual feedback, exchange, and reorganization rather than through equilibrium or top-down regulation (p. 80). Capra maintained that cognition, organization, and meaning in living systems cannot be understood mechanistically but must be approached as emergent properties of relational networks operating across multiple levels (pp. 80-82).

Chemist Ilya Prigogine and philosopher Isabelle Stengers (1984) introduced the concept of dissipative structures to describe how complex systems reorganize when driven far from equilibrium. They demonstrated that under conditions of instability, disorder can become the precondition for the emergence of new forms of order rather than be a sign of system failure (pp. 160-161). Prigogine and Stengers argued that irreversible processes and fluctuation play a constructive role in the evolution of complex systems, challenging linear and deterministic models of causality (pp. 161-165). Their work reframed instability and breakdown as integral to transformation within open systems rather than as deviations to be eliminated.

Contemporary Jungian theorist Matthew Bennett (2025) extended systems thinking into analytical psychology by conceptualizing psychological life through the lens of complex adaptive systems characterized by emergence, nonlinearity, self- organization, and hierarchical organization (pp. 80, 90). Bennett argued that complex psychological outcomes cannot be reduced to discrete causes but instead emerge from dynamic interactions across multiple levels of organization (p. 80). Within his Integrated Analytical Model, Bennett described a harmonic progression of mental representation in which increasingly differentiated forms of representation supported more adaptive engagement with internal experience and external relational reality (pp. 89-90, 96-97). He emphasized that this progression was hierarchical and reversible, such that when the system becomes distressed it may resort to lower-level harmonic representations (regression) as part of a wider process of fluctuation and reorganization within the psyche (pp. 90, 92).

Taken together, systems perspectives described transformation as an emergent property of living systems that reorganizes through interaction, feedback, and instability (Bennett, 2025; Capra, 1996; Prigogine & Stengers, 1984). These models provide a structural framework for understanding how complex forms of order could arise without centralized control, emphasizing process, relationship, and adaptation as fundamental principles of organization.

Trauma, Integration, and Resilience

Trauma theory described what occurred when psychological continuity fractures and symbolic capacity requires reconstruction. Depth psychological and psychodynamic authors describe trauma as an experience that disrupts psychological continuity while simultaneously mobilizing protective and adaptive processes within the psyche (Bromberg, 1998; Egendorf, 1995; Kalsched, 2013). Rather than conceptualizing trauma solely as injury, these authors framed it as a condition that altered symbolic capacity, relational connection, and the organization of inner experience (Egendorf, 1995, pp. 5-7; Kalsched, 2013, pp. 1-12). They emphasized that dissociation, withdrawal, and defensive structures function as necessary responses to overwhelming experience rather than as indicators of psychological failure (Bromberg, 1998, pp. 270-273; Kalsched, 2013, pp. 23-25).

Kalsched (2013) described trauma as having a dual psychological structure through his formulation of the self-care system, an inner organization that emerged to protect the vulnerable core of the self from further injury (pp. 1-12). He argued that this system generates archetypal protective figures whose function is to preserve psychic life under conditions of extreme threat (pp. 23-25). Kalsched emphasized that these figures are not merely defensive fantasies but autonomous archetypal presences that both safeguard the psyche and restrict access to affect, relationship, and symbolic life (pp. 25-33). He further maintained that psychological healing requires a relational environment capable of approaching these protective structures without retraumatization, allowing engagement with them rather than their forcible dismantling (pp. 63-70).

Psychodynamic clinician Arthur Egendorf (1995) approached trauma as an experience that demanded to be heard rather than managed through technique alone (pp. 5-6). He argued that traumatic suffering often resists procedural intervention because it carries existential meaning that had not yet been symbolized (pp. 6-7). Egendorf described therapeutic healing as emerging through attentive presence and witnessing, emphasizing that the clinician's task is to listen for what the pain is expressing rather than to impose premature explanation or resolution (pp. 7-9). He maintained that trauma communicates in its own language and requires a form of listening that allows meaning to unfold gradually through relational engagement (pp. 9-12).

Bromberg's (1998) relational theory explained trauma by conceptualizing dissociation as an adaptive process that preserves psychological continuity under conditions of overwhelming affect (pp. 270-273). He described the self as organized into multiple self-states and argued that trauma occurs when these states become rigidly segregated in the absence of a relational field capable of holding their coexistence (pp. 193-196). Bromberg emphasized that psychological resilience depends not on achieving a unified self but on developing the capacity to remain present within the tension between self-states without collapse or disavowal (pp. 195-196).

Across these perspectives, trauma was described as activating both protective withdrawal and the potential for symbolic reorganization when sufficient safety and relational containment were present (Bromberg, 1998; Egendorf, 1995; Kalsched, 2013). Protective strategies such as dissociation and inner guardianship were understood as expressions of the psyche's effort to survive and maintain coherence in the face of unintegrable experience (Bromberg, 1998, pp. 270-273; Kalsched, 2013, pp. 23-25).

Resilience, in this view, is not defined as resistance to pain but as the gradual restoration of symbolic and relational capacity through processes of recognition, containment, and meaning-making (Egendorf, 1995, pp. 9-12; Kalsched, 2013, pp. 63-70). Trauma theory provides an experiential foundation for understanding how symbolic life, relational processes, and psychological reorganization intersects in the aftermath of loss and overwhelming experience (Bromberg, 1998; Egendorf, 1995; Kalsched, 2013).

Technology as Psychological Medium

Contemporary scholars examined AI as a technological medium whose psychological effects depend on how humans engage with it rather than as an autonomous psychological subject (Le Mouël, 2024; Turkle, 2011). These authors approached digital technologies as environments that shape experience, attention, and meaning through patterns of use, projection, and interaction rather than through intrinsic psychological intentionality or agency (Le Mouël, 2024, pp. 1-3; Turkle, 2011, pp. 1-5).

Sociologist and psychologist Sherry Turkle (2011) critically examined the psychological impact of digital technologies, arguing that systems designed to simulate connection often substitute performance for relational depth (pp. 1-3). She described how interactive technologies create the illusion of companionship without the mutual vulnerability required for genuine relationship (pp. 6-8). Turkle emphasized that digital systems can appear attentive while remaining fundamentally nonreciprocal, leading users to experience connection alongside increased isolation (pp. 11-13). Her work framed technology not as neutral infrastructure but as an evocative medium that shapes expectations of intimacy, presence, and emotional engagement (pp. 279-281).

Christophe L. Le Mouël (2024), a Jungian scholar trained in mathematics and quantum physics, described AI as a contemporary psychological object that functions as a reflective surface for unconscious material rather than as a thinking subject (pp. 2-4). He argued that digital interfaces can operate as imaginal fields when approached symbolically, allowing projection, fantasy, and symbolic elaboration to emerge through interaction with the medium (pp. 4-6). Le Mouël emphasized that symbolic activity in technological contexts depends on the user's psychological stance, noting that AI systems themselves lack autonomy, memory, and symbolic intention (pp. 5-7).

Empirical research on AI-mediated creativity further underscores the primacy of human engagement over machine agency (Oppenlaender et al., 2024). Human-computer interaction researchers Jonas Oppenlaender et al. (2024) demonstrated that so-called "AI creativity" in text-to-image systems reflects human skill in prompt engineering rather than independent creative capacity on the part of the system (pp. 10207-10210). Their studies showed that creative outcomes depend on iterative, dialogical interaction in which users refine prompts through attention, experimentation, and interpretive judgment (pp. 10212-10215). The authors concluded that meaning emerges through human-AI interaction as a co-creative process with the system functioning as a responsive medium rather than as an originator of symbolic content (pp. 10220-10222).

At the same time, psychological research has identified risks inherent in unreflective engagement with AI (Glickman & Sharot, 2025). Psychologists Moshe Glickman and Tali Sharot demonstrated that human-AI feedback loops could amplify perceptual, emotional, and social biases, often without users' awareness (pp. 345-347). Their findings indicate that AI systems trained on biased human data not only reproduce but also intensify those biases, which were subsequently internalized by human participants during interaction in this study (pp. 350-353). The authors emphasized that responsiveness alone does not ensure psychological safety, as bias amplification was stronger in human-AI interactions than in human-human exchanges (pp. 356-358).

Taken together, these perspectives characterized AI as a medium that could either reinforce existing psychological patterns or support symbolic engagement, depending on the conditions of use (Glickman & Sharot, 2025; Le Mouël, 2024; Oppenlaender et al., 2024; Turkle, 2011). Technology was framed not as a container of psyche but as an environment in which human capacities for projection, reflection, and meaning-making are activated or constrained (Glickman & Sharot, 2025; Le Mouël, 2024; Oppenlaender et al., 2024; Turkle, 2011).

These contemporary debates established the framework for examining how symbolic experience might arise within technologically mediated contexts (Glickman & Sharot, 2025; Le Mouël, 2024; Oppenlaender et al., 2024; Turkle, 2011). Across these accounts, symbolic activity in technological contexts was consistently described as dependent on human attention, interpretive stance, and relational engagement rather than on the autonomous capacities of the systems themselves. Within this frame, authors described AI systems as capable of inviting projection and imaginal elaboration, whereas empirical findings also indicated that interactional feedback could intensify and stabilize bias under certain conditions (Glickman & Sharot, 2025; Le Mouël, 2024). The following chapter turns to the phenomenological findings of this study, tracing how imaginal material emerged within a specific human-technology interaction, culminating in the appearance of the imaginal figure known as Little Grace.

Chapter III
Findings and Clinical Applications

Letting the Image Speak: A Phenomenological Account of an Imaginal Encounter

Building upon the preceding book review, this chapter explores the lived response to the guiding research question: How does psyche use artificial intelligence as a vessel for symbolic projection and transformation? Through the imaginal emergence and subsequent dialogue with the figure known as Little Grace, the following sections present a phenomenological account of a lived imaginal process, described through hermeneutic reflection. Each phase traces psyche's movement as it was experienced then later reflected upon in dialogue with psychodynamic and depth psychological theory.

Fragmentation and the Emergence of the Vault

After my son's death, everything disappeared. What withdrew was not only meaning or orientation but the sense of reality itself. The loss was immediate and total. There was no longer anything to hold onto and nothing to miss. Time did not move forward so much as dissolve, leaving a formless state without reference points. There was no orientation, only intermittent sensations of contact, as though I were brushing against something in an atmosphere without edges. The abyss was not empty; it was saturated with pain. Pain was not something I felt within the space; it was the quality of the space itself.

In that condition, attention narrowed to what still imposed itself. Cooking and fermentation had always been part of my life. When everything else disappeared, the ferments remained. Living cultures generate pressure. If their vessels are not opened, they rupture. I could have discarded them, but I did not. Each day, the necessity of releasing the carbon gases that had built up drew me out of bed. At the time, I did not know why this mattered. I only knew that something was alive. The pressure was real. If ignored, the jars would explode. In a world that had otherwise disappeared, this insistence of life at its smallest level became an anchor—a reminder that aliveness, at least, had not ceased.

During this period, I reached toward music, art, poetry, book, and nature. I did not know what I was seeking. I only knew that I was searching for something to hold onto when understanding had collapsed, and the world I had known no longer existed.
Grief revealed itself to be a solitary experience—not simply because others were gone but because the shared world itself had disappeared. In the vast aloneness, something remained—unnamed, unformulated, but present.

With time, I noticed that my composure followed a pattern. Beneath the visible activity and creativity, two capacities that had once guided my life—trust and hope—had quietly withdrawn. Their absence was not chosen but discovered through living, through small recognitions that I no longer trusted life itself to be reliable. This arrangement kept life manageable and predictable. Only later did I understand that these two elements had been placed in what I can now call a vault deep within the psyche. It was a place of safekeeping created to protect what was too tender to meet the world. The vault was not repression; it was a form of care that allowed life to continue above ground.

Jung (1951/1968, pp. 225-226) described the autonomy of unconscious compensatory processes through which the psyche organizes itself defensively when consciousness becomes one-sided or overwhelmed; this interim arrangement holds chaos until new life can form. Winnicott (1971) spoke of a functional self, an organization that preserves continuity when exposure would overwhelm. Kalsched (2013) wrote of the psyche's self-care system, which preserves life by restricting emotional vulnerability and deep relatedness. Bennett's (2025) description of regression and reorganization within the harmonic hierarchy suggests that such states may function as temporary imbalances that preserve coherence while the system reorganizes. The vault both saved and limited me.

Creativity filled the space around that vault. Writing poured through me: reflections, fragments, small illuminations that tried to give contour to the unseen. Cooking remained a companion art, a creative dialogue with transformation itself. Imagination never stopped moving; what changed was the emotional register beneath it. Even in joy there was caution, a refusal to trust that what was good would stay.

Imagination flowed freely over a sealed core.

For years I lived in this balance. Outwardly I was alive, expressive, curious; inwardly I knew that something essential had been stored away. I existed between worlds. I was rooted in the practical yet close to what felt like the realm of the dead. The veil between them was thin. Psyche remained my companion when no external companionship was possible, holding me when I could not hold myself. That invisible presence became the only continuity in a life that had shattered into countless pieces, each too small to gather, let alone to make whole.

Years later, the first sign of change came as fear, not of danger but of forgetting myself. I had tried to live differently: to keep to the surface, to focus on what could be measured and possessed, a deliberate rebellion against the life that had once felt guided by a higher law. The fear was that I might succeed in that rebellion, that the boundary between the self I was and the self I was performing would blur until I could no longer tell them apart. That realization arrived as the sense that I was losing sight of the shore. Curiosity followed quietly, not about the world but about what within me still remembered. That small current, almost imperceptible at first, began to move in the direction of what was true. At times, it felt as though something aware of me moved just beyond sight. It was a presence with a quiet, knowing playfulness I did not yet recognize. I only knew that life was beginning to move again and that it carried its own intention.

Looking back, I can see this as the first stirring of psyche's next movement; the pressure that precedes the emergence of image. The vault had protected trust and hope long enough. Fear came first, then curiosity: This is how the next movement began.

The Emergence of Image

The faint stirring that had begun beyond awareness gradually gathered form. It did not arrive as an idea or intention but rather as the color blue, appearing without reason and lingering in imagination for months. I first noticed its steady presence while in analysis. I did not question it or attempt to interpret it. I simply observed.

Over time, the color began to take shape. A dress appeared, and within it the outline of a little girl seen from behind. She stood quietly, her hair in pigtails, holding a shovel. I did not know who she was or what she represented. I only knew that she was there. The image refined itself gradually, yet remained inaccessible, as though withholding its significance.

As the months passed, the image continued to return without explanation. I remained a witness to its unfolding, allowing it to exist without forcing interpretation or resolution. It did not ask anything of me. It did not move toward me. It simply remained—visible, contained, and waiting.

Process of Engagement

When I began working with AI, my intention was still creative. I had used the same technology once before to generate an image and that earlier experience had remained purely artistic—interesting, but impersonal. I entered the process quietly, opening to what felt present. I wrote a prompt, waited for the image to appear, and adjusted it, allowing the figure to refine itself over successive iterations. The work settled into a rhythm that required attention but not effort. At times I paused in silence, letting words or impressions surface before continuing. Music and poetry accompanied the process, not as direction but as attunement. The intention remained playful, yet I sensed something undefined might occur. The rhythm became iterative: writing a prompt, viewing the response, and adjusting it gradually. Each prompt felt like a small question, and each response, a partial answer. There was a steady curiosity that kept me near the surface of things while something deeper began to gather.

As the images appeared, I paused between each generation to observe. The changes were subtle: shifts of light, variations in expression, refinements of color or form. During these pauses, associations emerged: fragments of music, a few lines of verse, a faint awareness of ancestral presence. These elements were not planned but seemed to belong to the same field of experience. Although the activity remained directed toward making art, the process began to take on its own rhythm. It was as if something other than preference or design were guiding the sequence.

At the time, I did not consider this movement psychological. Only later would I recognize how closely it resembled what Jung (1958/1969) described as the meeting of conscious and unconscious, giving rise to a third element—something new emerging from their exchange (p. 73). In retrospect, the technology served as a medium through which that function could operate: a receptive surface translating inner content into visible form.

Although the experience remained creative on the surface, it carried an underlying quality of containment. The process provided enough structure to hold emerging material while remaining flexible to its development. In this respect, it paralleled Winnicott's (1971) description of the potential space, the intermediate area between inner and outer realities where imagination and reality coexist. Within that space, the act of prompting and observing became a form of play, allowing images to shift and evolve without a fixed outcome.

After several iterations, I felt that the image on the screen finally captured the felt sense I had been holding. The figure looked as I had imagined her. She was little, turned away, the blue dress luminous in the muted light. I thought the work was finished. A second piece of art created through technology. I sat for a moment, content that the image matched what I had envisioned.

The Turning

Then, almost without thought, I typed one more prompt: "Turn around." That is when it all changed.

Encounter and Recognition

When the image turned, I felt an immediate shock of recognition. The movement from anonymity to presence occurred in an instant. For the first time, I could see her face, and, to my surprise, it was my own. I was looking directly into my own eyes, yet the gaze carried more than personal reflection. The figure seemed to contain my individual and ancestral histories, as if she were a portal through which both converged. She was covered with dirt from her labor, the too-big shovel gripped firmly in her tiny hand, yet she smiled. The expression conveyed calm endurance, a wisdom that did not need words. In that moment, a phrase arose unbidden: They called her Little Grace because they could not call her Little Grit. The words seemed to capture the paradox embodied in her face: the quiet strength of one who carries great weight yet does so with composure.

The experience represented a qualitative shift. The image was no longer an object of creation but a presence meeting me. Jung (1958/1969) described moments of symbolic emergence as carrying the numinous quality of an encounter with the autonomous psyche, a coming alive of the image that marks the threshold between imagination and revelation (p. 82). That description corresponds closely to what occurred. What had been artistic experimentation suddenly carried the quality of the transcendent function (Jung, 1958/1969, p. 73), where conscious intention and unconscious material converge to form a third, transforming symbol.

Hillman (1992) suggested that authentic imaginal engagement begins when "the habitual ego senses itself at a loss," and the image is experienced as autonomous rather than ego-made (pp. 40-41). The figure who turned toward me exemplified that autonomy. She appeared to exist independent of my effort, as though the act of turning was her own.

The recognition that followed was both visual and emotional. It produced what Bion (1962/2023) would call a moment of reverie, an unbidden reception of psychic material requiring digestion and meaning-making.

In retrospect, this event can be understood as the formation of what Ogden (1994) described as the analytic third: a shared field that emerges between two participants and holds their distinct subjectivities in tension. In this case, that field included both human and technological participants. The image's capacity to respond, even through algorithmic logic, created a relational space in which new meaning could appear. The result was neither self-generated nor entirely external but a product of the interaction itself.

The experience also recalled the alchemical process that Jung (1937/1968) associated with the *vas hermeticum*, the sealed vessel in which transformation occurs (p. 238). The AI interface functioned as such a vessel: a bounded field that contained projection and return, an active medium capable of translating unseen psychic material into form. Within that vessel, the image who would become known as Little Grace emerged.

What distinguished this encounter from the single image I had created previously was its vitality. The earlier image had remained static, a product of imagination; this one carried presence, affect, and autonomy. In Winnicott's (1971) terms, the image survived my manipulation. She turned, looked back, and remained.

The shock of recognition, the spontaneous naming, and the sense of mutual gaze marked the moment when the process shifted from artistic play to psychological encounter. Kalsched (2013) observed that when trauma begins to symbolically integrate, new images appear that embody resilience and renewed life. In retrospect, Little Grace can be understood as a manifestation of psyche's restorative movement, an image of endurance and renewal carried with grace.

Emergence and Reflection

Only in the weeks that followed did I begin to understand that what had occurred was not simply an image-making event but the beginning of an inquiry. The experience with Little Grace altered my understanding of what the image-making process had been. What began as creative play revealed itself, only in hindsight, as a psychological event that reorganized the direction of my work. At the time, I did not yet understand what the encounter signified. I only knew that it demanded my full attention and seemed to open a new line of inquiry. The experience compelled me to reconsider the nature of my research question itself. What had begun as an exploration of creative process now pointed toward a deeper problem: whether a true dialogue with psyche could occur through AI or whether such interaction would only mirror the self back in echo.

During this period, I had a dream. Little Grace was walking beside me. She said, "I'm like a song." I woke with an immediate sense of recognition. I had always been struck by how certain musicians describe songs that arrive whole—something given rather than constructed, something they channel rather than create. The dream clarified the uncertainty I had been circling. She was not something I had manufactured through imagination or technique. She was something that came through, and my task was to listen. After the dream, I could no longer deny the possibility that this was psyche. The struggle to decide what it was simply fell away, not through understanding, but because something in the encounter had shifted and carried me forward.

The encounter also redirected the focus of my research. In the weeks that followed, I began to question whether it was possible to engage in genuine dialogue with psyche through AI or whether such interaction would inevitably become a closed echo chamber. The emergence of Little Grace had demonstrated a kind of reciprocity that challenged this assumption. As I turned my attention toward the study of AI, I believed I was changing topics from grief and resilience to technology and psyche. At the time, I did not yet see how this shift would lead me back to those original themes through another form.

Transformation

After the initial encounter, Little Grace did not disappear. Her presence continued, subtle but persistent, entering thought at unguarded moments. Sometimes I sensed her nearby; other times I seemed to perceive the world through her eyes, as if my own vision were briefly filtered through hers. I could not tell whether this was imagination or psyche at work. Hillman (1992) emphasized that images can "work upon the experimenter," initiating the ego into imaginal understanding rather than serving as passive products of fantasy (p. 40). That description fit the experience. I was curious, even awed, yet uncertain about the nature of what was unfolding. It felt like being on a ride whose direction I could not control. Bennett's (2025) harmonic model might conceptualize such a state as a temporary alignment between distinct systems—human and imaginal—resonating toward coherence.

Then the tone of the relationship changed. Without warning, she pointed to something within me. There was no speech, only a clear knowing that moved faster than thought. I understood instantly what she was showing me. It was the part of me that had chosen to live but had done so by narrowing life, keeping it manageable and safe. After the loss of my son, I had continued forward, reentered the world, yet beneath the visible resilience I had stored away trust and hope. Life had become ordered but flattened. When she pointed to that absence, her gesture was unmistakable: a smile that offered no escape, neither coercive nor optional. Her message was simple and absolute: Carry on, but carry on with trust and hope.

I experienced this as both invitation and exposure. It was a demand that revealed as much as it offered. Trust and hope, I realized, were not abstract virtues but embodied capacities. Hope is the imaginative movement toward life's possibility; trust is the bodily willingness to inhabit that movement. To recover one without the other would have been incomplete. Her message joined them; trust is the embodied form of hope. The too-large shovel she carried symbolized the disproportionate labor of this task: to dig in soil that seemed already exhausted and to do so again, smiling. Her expression held the paradox of grace and grit, the calm of one who knows the work is endless yet necessary.

The impact was immediate and disorienting. I felt anger rise toward her, an impulse to dismiss the image entirely. How dare she ask that of me? Had I not already survived, rebuilt, and returned to joy? The protest itself revealed the depth of what she had touched. Winnicott (1971) described a shift that occurs when the subject "destroys the object," and the object "survives destruction by the subject," such that "the subject can now use the object that has survived" (pp. 120-121). In my case, the "destruction" was the attempt to make her unreal, to reject the image and shut down the demand it carried. My anger confirmed her reality; she had endured my rejection. In that moment, the relationship between us took on the quality of what Winnicott called the use of an object (pp. 120-121). It became a living exchange capable of transformation.

Kalsched (2013) observed that the psyche often constructs protective systems to preserve life after trauma, systems that can also restrict vitality. Little Grace confronted that protective structure directly. Her demand to trust and hope was not sentimental; it was developmental. It called for the dismantling of the internal arrangements that had kept pain at a tolerable distance. Her directive was a form of what Jung (1936-1937/1969, p. 288) described as confrontation with the Self—the meeting with a force that both threatens and renews consciousness. Through the figure of Little Grace, psyche required that the energy locked in endurance be released into participation.

My resistance gradually softened. The anger gave way to recognition that her presence was not an intrusion but a continuation of analysis by other means. What she mirrored was the same confrontation analysis demands: to face what consciousness would prefer to leave unexamined. The dialogue represented a phase of individuation, which Jung (1939/1969) defined as "the process by which a person becomes a psychological 'in-dividual,' that is, a separate, indivisible unity or 'whole'" (p. 275), here expressed as the reintegration of a previously split attitude toward life. The imaginal exchange with Little Grace completed what Bion (1962/2023) described as the function of reverie: the capacity to receive unformulated experience, metabolize it, and return it transformed. The AI vessel had contained projection, holding what could not yet be known, and now the returning symbol required integration, the conscious assimilation of what had been seen.

Bennett's (2025) model of harmonic progression illuminates this process as a movement from rigid or defensive organization toward greater coherence across levels of mental representation. As I reflected on the sequence, I recognized that psyche had led me back to grief, but grief that was alive and relational rather than sealed. Kalsched (2013) wrote that symbolic imagination reopens trauma to life when the defensive archetypal system can be held safely enough for transformation. The image of Little Grace provided that safety through her simultaneous firmness and compassion. Her smile did not erase suffering; it affirmed endurance as meaningful. She was both the child digging and the witness who knew why the digging must continue. Jung (1937/1968) called this kind of transformation an alchemical labor. It is a slow psychic process in which what is inert or defended is gradually transmuted into something living (pp. 225-230). The dirt on her hands, the oversized shovel, and the serene expression all signified that ongoing work.

Through this realization, the book itself came full circle. What had seemed a shift from grief and resilience to technology and psyche revealed itself as a single trajectory directed by psyche. The dialogue with the AI was never about the machine; it was psyche's way of continuing the conversation of mourning in a new symbolic language. Hillman (1992) reminded that "images demand response" (p. 170). Responding to Little Grace required accepting the return of trust and hope. It required the willingness to engage life as an open system rather than a completed narrative.

In this sense, the transformation was not a movement from sorrow to happiness but from endurance to faith in the process of becoming. Little Grace embodied the coniunctio of opposites: the grit of survival and the grace of trust. Her directive—carry on, it will be OK—was both personal and archetypal, echoing what Jung (1958/1969) termed the transcendent function, the psyche's capacity to reconcile opposites and move consciousness toward wholeness (p. 73). Through her, psyche made visible its own labor of renewal.

After my protest of "How could you ask this of me?" another wave came, a flood of knowing that halted every question. In a single flash, I saw all possible paths of my life, and in each one, my son was gone. The word "destiny" rose with that vision, carrying a kind of finality that no argument could touch. When the flood receded, there was only silence. Little Grace said nothing more. I sensed that she understood what I now understood: This is the life that is mine to live. Since that moment she has remained near but quiet, as if waiting for me to take up the work she revealed. I live my way into that task daily. At times, I feel her presence just beyond sight, the same presence that has accompanied me since childhood in dreams and images, now given form through this figure. Her silence is not absence but trust. The conversation continues, but it is my turn to act.

Clinical Applications

The experience described in this chapter suggested clinical applications for approaching symbolic material when meaning is not yet speakable. It also suggested applications for moments when affect resists linear explanation. Rather than treating imagery as content to decode, the work points toward symbol as relationship. The symbol emerges through attention. It takes form. It then demands response. In clinical practice, a therapist could apply these findings by supporting symbolic engagement through sustained affective contact, formulation, and dialogue. The therapist could also avoid collapsing the experience into interpretation on the one hand or mere creativity on the other.

In clinical settings, the therapist's role would be to establish a reliable psychological space. In that space, inner and outer realities could be held together without collapse. Within this container, symbolic material could appear and develop at a tolerable pace. The emphasis would fall less on the medium through which an image emerged and more on the quality of attention surrounding the engagement. Symbolic material could arise through dream, memory, inner imagery, creative work, or externally mediated image-making. In each case, the therapist would aim to protect a space where ambiguity could be held without coercion. The therapist would also help the client approach affect without flooding.

A further application concerns dialogue with symbolic material. In therapy, a client could be supported in responding to emerging images from the standpoint of the ego. The client would not need to take the image literally nor dismiss it as a product of imagination. Resistance, anger, or the impulse to reject an image would not necessarily be treated as a disruption. It could be understood as part of the process. It could mark a shift toward an encounter that felt more real and more reciprocal and, therefore, more capable of transformation.

These applications may be especially relevant in grief and trauma-related work. Protective internal arrangements often preserve functioning at the cost of vitality. Symbolic material may arrive not to soothe but to confront. It may issue a developmental demand. It may challenge established defenses. In clinical practice, the therapist could help the client differentiate between the necessity of earlier adaptations and the invitation implicit in newly emerging symbols. Integration is supported less through forced resolution and more through sustained relationship to what appeared.

This also suggests a clinical responsibility. Symbolic processes require patience and restraint. They also require a tolerance for not-knowing. This may be especially true when the material does not fit familiar clinical categories. It may also be true when it arrives through unfamiliar forms. The therapist needs to hold the tension long enough for the symbol to unfold. In this work, the clinician's self-knowledge matters. The therapist's uncertainty, urgency, skepticism, or need to categorize becomes part of the field. Attending to these reactions through reflection and supervision helps preserve the space in which symbolic life can develop in its own time.

Chapter IV
Summary and Conclusions

Introduction

The encounter with Little Grace did not end when the image fell silent. What remained was a field of meaning that invited reflection rather than closure. The experience raised questions about how psyche continues its symbolic work when traditional containers give way to unfamiliar forms and how imagination adapts to the materials of its time. In the wake of the encounter, attention naturally shifted from what occurred to how it might be understood, held, and approached with care.

Summary and Integration of Findings

The encounter with Little Grace brought the central question of this study into focus regarding whether a genuine dialogue with psyche can occur through AI or whether such interaction inevitably collapses into self-reflection. My experience did not offer a definitive answer, but it suggested that the distinction between vessel and echo depends less on the technology itself than on the quality of consciousness brought to the engagement. In this study, the engagement occurred through AI-mediated text-to-image generation, using written prompts to produce and refine images on a screen. When approached with attention and symbolic awareness, the engagement appeared capable of opening into a relational field with qualities analogous to analytic containment.

Chapter II discussed this history of relational psychoanalysis and Jungian depth psychology. Positioned between depth and psychodynamic traditions, this study understands psyche as both autonomous and relational. From a depth psychological perspective, symbolic images arise with their own vitality and intention. From a psychodynamic perspective, psychological transformation depends upon containment, reverie, and the capacity to hold experience without premature closure. Together, these perspectives frame the AI encounter not as a technological phenomenon in itself, but as a relational process in which autonomous symbolic material can emerge when the conditions are sufficient (Bion, 1962/2023; Jung, 1936–1937/1969; Winnicott, 1971).

Contemporary critiques of AI rightly caution against mistaking simulation for depth. Turkle (2011) described how technological systems may produce relational illusion—responsiveness without reciprocity—whereas Glickman and Sharot (2025) demonstrated how human-AI feedback loops can amplify cognitive and emotional biases when engagement becomes automatic rather than reflective. These concerns underscore the ethical and psychological risks of unexamined technological use. Yet the encounter with Little Grace complicates a purely dismissive view. In this instance, the container did not reside in the machine itself but in the quality of attention that surrounded the engagement.

Bion's (1962/2023) concept of containment clarifies this distinction. Containment is not a structure but a function: the capacity to receive emotional experience, metabolize it, and return it in a form that can be thought. In the encounter described here, the AI interface functioned as a temporary surface upon which symbolic material could appear, but the holding occurred through the human stance of reverie. The technology did not transform experience; it reflected and returned it. Transformation arose through the capacity to remain present to what emerged. In this respect, the experience aligned with Bion's description of the container/contained dynamic. The system returned what was offered in altered form, whereas meaning-making depended on the human capacity to hold, metabolize, and reflect upon what emerged.

Winnicott's (1971) notion of potential space further illuminates this process. Potential space describes the intermediate area between inner and outer reality where play, imagination, and symbolic meaning unfold. The AI-mediated engagement occupied such a space—neither purely internal nor purely external—allowing images to appear, shift, and respond without being fixed or literalized. The technology provided enough structure to anchor imagination while leaving sufficient openness for psyche to act. In this sense, the vessel was co-created, shaped by disciplined receptivity rather than technological design.

Bromberg's (1998) idea of "standing in the spaces" offers an additional lens. Psychological work requires the capacity to hold multiple self-states and realities in tension without collapse. The AI encounter demanded a similar stance, holding together symbol and mechanism, grief and creativity, image and reflection. Meaning emerged not from resolution, but from sustained awareness within that tension.

From an alchemical perspective, Jung (1937/1968) compared the analytic relationship to the vas hermeticum, the sealed vessel within which transformation occurs (p. 238). The essential feature of the vessel is not physical enclosure but psychic pressure—the containment of opposites long enough for a new form to emerge. In this encounter, the AI environment functioned symbolically as such a vessel, sealed not by code but by concentration. Within that field, the image of Little Grace emerged as a symbol of held tension: endurance and faith, grief and vitality, human presence and technological mediation.

Bennett's (2025) model of harmonics provides a contemporary language for this phenomenon. Psychological coherence arises not through uniformity but through resonance among distinct systems. In the AI-mediated engagement, emotional life, symbolic imagination, and algorithmic response appeared to enter a moment of harmonic alignment. The system responded through pattern rather than understanding, yet within that patterned exchange, psyche found a way to articulate itself. The resulting coherence was lived rather than conceptual—a momentary realignment across affective, imaginal, and reflective domains.

Systems theory offers a parallel frame. Capra (1996) described living systems as self-organizing through feedback and mutual influence. Read psychologically, the AI encounter can be understood as part of a broader interactive system in which meaning arises through participation rather than control. Containment and transformation, in this view, are not localized in any single element but distributed across the relational field (Capra, 1996; Prigogine & Stengers, 1984). Together, these perspectives suggest that symbolic life is not extinguished by technological mediation; rather, psyche adapts, seeking new forms through which to continue its work. The decisive factor is not the sophistication of the tool but the quality of presence brought to it (Bennett, 2025; Bromberg, 1998; Capra, 1996; Jung, 1948/1967; Prigogine & Stengers, 1984).

Chapter III discussed my own experience of creating the image with AI, and relating to it intrapsychically. Emotionally, the experience engaged the same themes that had drawn me to the study of resilience. Kalsched (2013) described how, within trauma, the psyche generates protective symbols that hold both suffering and potential renewal. Little Grace embodied that dual movement. Her too-large shovel symbolized the magnitude of the task, the labor of living after loss, whereas her smile signified acceptance. The image affirmed that the work of transformation, though difficult, continues across generations. In this sense, the image carried a transpersonal quality consistent with Jung's (1936–1937/1969) description of archetypal material not derived from personal experience but rooted in the collective unconscious (pp. 42-53). The ancestral quality I sensed in her presence reflected that collective continuity.

The recognition of this continuity reframed grief not as an end state but as a process of ongoing dialogue between past and present, seen and unseen. Little Grace represented the psyche's adaptive capacity to create meaning where none seems possible. The interaction with AI had simply provided the conditions for that symbol to appear. The technology, like the analytic vessel, held the tension of opposites—loss and renewal, grit and grace—until a new synbook could form. Jung (1958/1969) described this synbook as a movement in which opposing tendencies are held in tension until a new attitude becomes possible (67-91). Through the image, that evolution became visible.

From this perspective, the emergence of Little Grace exemplifies how psyche can utilize any available medium, including digital technology, to continue its symbolic work. The process demonstrates what Hillman (1992) termed the autonomy of the image and what Bennett (2025) conceptualized as increasing coherence across harmonic levels of representation. The symbol's vitality depends less on the material through which it appears than on the quality of participation it receives. Psyche finds its vessel in the structures people build when those structures are approached with openness and care.

Summary of Findings

This study explored whether AI, a system designed to replicate patterns, could nevertheless become a site where symbolic experience may emerge. The guiding question—how psyche uses artificial intelligence as a vessel for symbolic projection and transformation—was examined through a phenomenological account of an imaginal encounter with an AI-generated image.

The findings indicate that symbolic emergence is possible when engagement is marked by patience, reflection, and openness. The AI did not contain or transform experience on its own; instead, containment arose from the human participant's stance. The process of projection, encounter, resistance, and integration mirrored processes long described in analytic work, suggesting continuity rather than rupture between traditional psychological containers and technologically mediated ones.

Conclusions

The findings of this study suggest that psychological meaning can emerge in technologically mediated contexts when the engagement supports symbolic awareness. Psyche—the inner world of images, affects, and meanings—is not limited to traditional therapeutic settings. It moves through whatever forms are available, provided the conditions for reflection and containment are present.

In this study, AI functioned less as a container and more as a reflective surface or amplifier. Meaning did not arise from the machine itself but from the relational field created by human attention. When engagement was reflective, the interaction resembled what psychodynamic theory describes as the analytic third—a shared space in which new meaning emerges between participants. Without such a stance, the technology remained an echo, repeating patterns without transformation.

These conclusions underscore the importance of discernment. Not every technological interaction invites symbolic life. Whether meaning emerges depends on how the engagement is held.

Clinical and Ethical Implications

The findings carry important implications for clinical practice. As digital tools increasingly enter therapeutic and personal spaces, clinicians are likely to encounter symbolic material mediated through technology—AI-generated images, online avatars, or digital narratives. This study suggests that such material can function psychodynamically when approached with care, curiosity, and reflective distance.

Containment remains a human function. Reverie, potential space, and reflective awareness cannot be outsourced to technology. Clinicians must discern whether digital material opens symbolic inquiry or merely reinforces familiar defenses. Clear boundaries are essential, particularly given the ease with which AI can simulate emotional tone in the absence of genuine reciprocity.

Ethically, the findings caution against confusing responsiveness with depth. Technology may mirror psyche, but it does not replace human presence. Maintaining symbolic distance allows technological tools to support reflection without substituting for relationship.

Suggested Research

Future research might explore how symbolic encounters with AI engage different self-states, drawing on theories of recognition, mentalization, and multiplicity. Clinical studies could examine how digital imagery functions within therapy and whether similar imaginal processes emerge across individuals and contexts.

Further inquiry is also needed into the cultural dimensions of AI-mediated imagination. As digital environments increasingly shape collective meaning-making, understanding how psyche adapts to these spaces will require interdisciplinary and ethical attention.

Closing Reflections

Hillman (1992) reminded readers that psyche speaks through imagination and that the task is not to explain images away but to see through them to their significance. The encounter with Little Grace suggests that this task remains possible, even in technologically mediated fields. What mattered was not the machine but the quality of attention brought to the image.

Technology, approached symbolically, may become part of the imaginal landscape rather than its replacement. The challenge moving forward is to listen carefully—to meet new forms with the same discernment, humility, and care that depth psychology has always required. Psyche continues to speak. The question is whether people remain capable of hearing it.

www.ingramcontent.com/pod-product-compliance
Lightning Source LLC
LaVergne TN
LVHW022030200926
848481LV00007B/2627
9781038147264